VIOLIN
PLAY-ALONG

AUDIO
ACCESS
INCLUDED

PLAYBACK+
Speed • Pitch • Balance • Loop

ROCK CLASSICS

To access audio visit:
www.halleonard.com/mylibrary
Enter Code
5613-1726-6401-8247

ISBN 978-1-4950-2999-8

HAL•LEONARD®
CORPORATION
7777 W. BLUEMOUND RD. P.O. BOX 13819 MILWAUKEE, WI 53213

In Australia Contact:
Hal Leonard Australia Pty. Ltd.
4 Lenatara Court
Cheltenham, 3192 Victoria, Australia
Email: ausadmin@halleonard.com.au

Visit Hal Leonard Online at
www.halleonard.com

Jerry Loughney, violin
Angela Schmidt, cello
Tom Crowell, electric and acoustic guitar
Dan Maske, keyboards, percussion, bass

Arranged, Recorded, and Produced by Dan Maske

CONTENTS

4   Danse Macabre
    SAINT-SAËNS

9   Eine kleine Nachtmusik
    MOZART

12 Hungarian Dance No. 5
    BRAHMS

14 In the Hall of the Mountain King
    GRIEG

16 Jesu, Joy of Man's Desiring
    J.S. BACH

18 Mars (from *The Planets*)
    HOLST

22 Symphony No. 5 in C Minor
    (First Movement)
    BEETHOVEN

26 William Tell Overture
    ROSSINI

Danse Macabre

By Camille Saint-Saëns

Eine kleine Nachtmusik

By Wolfgang Amadeus Mozart

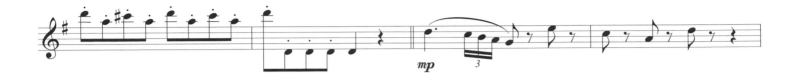

Hungarian Dance No. 5

By Johannes Brahms

Spirited Rock

Half-time feel

let ring

Optional 8va on repeat

Optional 8va on repeat

Fast Rock

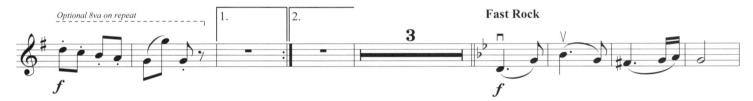

Slower

rit.

a tempo

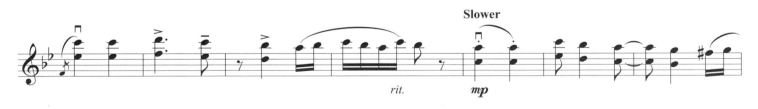

In the Hall of the Mountain King

from PEER GYNT
By Edvard Grieg

accel.

Briskly

accel.

Very fast

Jesu, Joy of Man's Desiring

Music by Johann Sebastian Bach

Mars

from THE PLANETS
By Gustav Holst

Half time

5

a tempo (double time)

Symphony No. 5 in C Minor

First Movement Excerpt
By Ludwig Van Beethoven

William Tell Overture

By G. Rossini